A Family in India

LIBRARY OF CONGRESS CATALOGING IN PUBLICATION DATA

Tigwell, Tony.
  A family in India.

  Original title: Sakina in India.
  Summary: Ten-year-old Sakina talks about her life
in a northern Indian village.
  1. India—Social life and customs—Juvenile literature.
2. Family—India—Juvenile literature. [1. India—Social
life and customs] I. Title.
DS421.T55 1985   306'.0954   84-19446
ISBN 0-8225-1654-3 (lib. bdg.)

Manufactured in the United States of America

3   4   5   6   7   8   9   10   94   93   92   91   90

A Family in India

Tony Tigwell

Lerner Publications Company • Minneapolis

Sakina is 10. She lives in Taku-kibowli, a village in northern India. Her village is not far from Varanasi (also known as Benares), a famous city on the Ganges River.

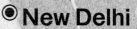**New Delhi**

UTTAR

Sakina lives with her family, which includes her father, Karam Ali, her mother, Sabun Nisi Bibi, and her brother, Asharap, who is 6. They are standing in front of their house.

Sakina's mother is wearing a cotton *sari*, but Sakina is wearing her *shalwar* (baggy trousers), *kameez* (tunic), and *dupatta* (scarf).

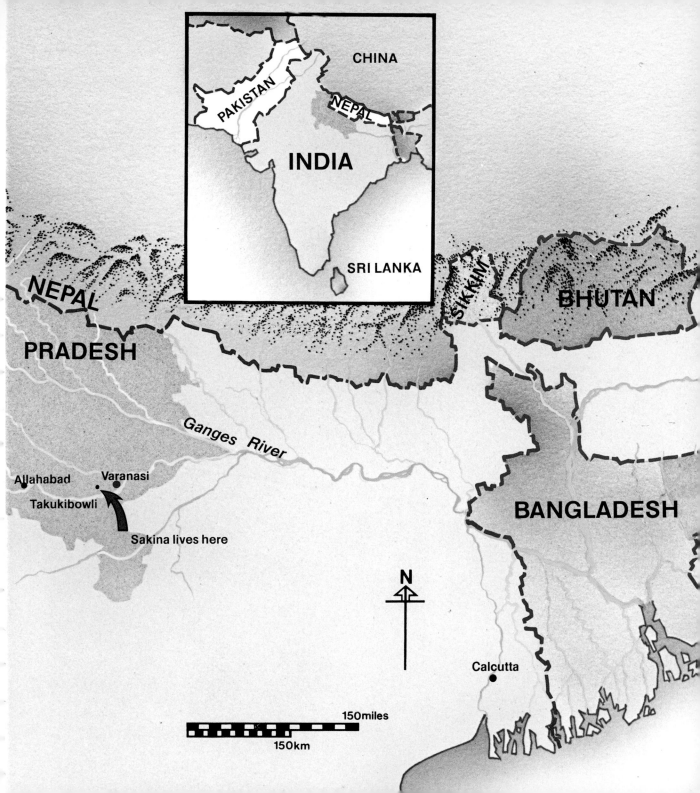

CHINA

PAKISTAN

NEPAL

INDIA

SRI LANKA

NEPAL

PRADESH

SIKKIM

BHUTAN

BANGLADESH

Ganges River

Allahabad

Varanasi

Takukibowli

Sakina lives here

N

Calcutta

150 miles

150 km

The family speaks the Hindi language, and Sakina is learning to write Hindi at school. She dips a bamboo pen into white ink made with chalk and writes words on a black wooden slate. It's easy to wash the letters off and begin again.

Asharap and Sakina walk to school at about 8:00 A.M., after their breakfast of hot cereal and sugar cane juice. Sakina's friend Shushma comes from her house to meet them.

Sometimes Shushma picks fresh chick-peas on her way and shares them with her friends as they walk to school.

Although Asharap is four years younger than Sakina, he is only one year behind her in school. That is because Sakina doesn't always go to school. Her parents often keep her at home to help around the house.

At school, the students sit in straight lines. The teacher is very strict. The class studies the history and geography of India and also learns arithmetic. Sakina and her brother come home from school at noon. In the afternoons, the teacher has a different class.

Sakina's house is located alongside the main road at one end of the village. In the center of the village, there are shops selling tea, salt, oil, batteries, cloth, and many other things. One man sells crackers, peanuts, and salty snacks from a hand cart. People from nearby villages often come to Takukibowli to do their shopping.

No one in the village has a car, but many of the men own bicycles. Sakina's father has a bicycle that was made in India. Indian bicycles are built to be very strong because the roads are so uneven.

During the winter when the sun isn't too hot, Sakina and her family enjoy sitting in front of their house. They watch people traveling along the road. Sometimes the express bus to Allahabad goes by. When the bus passes their house, it covers everyone with dust.

Sakina's father and neighbors built their house. It is made of bricks and clay. The bricks are made at a kiln in the village. Young girls work at the kiln and carry heavy loads on their heads. The tiles on the roof of the house were made by a local potter.

Sakina's family is Muslim. When anyone comes to see them, they say *"Asalaam alaicum,"* which means "God bless you." Theirs is the only Muslim family in the village. The other families are all Hindu.

One of Sakina's neighbors is Balukhnibai. She works with her husband in the fields. The earth is very hard, so she uses a *powra* for digging. It has a blade and is used like a pick.

Balukhnibai's husband is plowing one of the fields near their house. He uses young bulls to pull the plow and prods them with a stick when they stop. When the field is plowed, he will plant chick-peas.

Most of the people in Takukibowli are farmers. They grow wheat, sugar cane, lentils, and vegetables.

Both of Sakina's parents work at home. Her father is a weaver. There are two looms in the front room of the house, set into pits in the clay floor. Her father sits on a plank with his feet on the pedals. He and his friend, Balikaran, begin work as soon as it is light. Each day Sakina and her brother wake up to the "clack-clack" sound of the looms.

Balikaran and Sakina's father weave borders which are cut up and sewn onto *saris*. They sell the borders for eight rupees a meter. A meter is slightly longer than a yard. Sakina's father weaves about six meters a day. The family can buy a bar of soap for one rupee or an aluminum cooking pot for eight rupees.

The silver thread that her father uses is expensive, so he works carefully. The shuttle that weaves in and out of the threads is made of polished buffalo horn. It must be smooth or it will tear the fine threads.

Lots of wire and string lead from each loom to a box above it. Balikaran is fixing a set of cards into the box above his loom. The cards have holes punched in them. Each set of cards adjusts the loom to weave a different pattern.

The wooden frame for the loom was made by a carpenter in Takukibowli. Here the carpenter uses an adze, which is a kind of ax, to shape part of a new frame for a loom.

Sakina's father was trained as a weaver at Sevapuri Ashram, which is less than two miles (three kilometers) from Takukibowli. The ashram has several workshops where people can learn to make tiles, soap, matches, and other useful things. One of the people who trained Sakina's father is Iqbal Singh, shown here standing near one of the workshops.

An ashram is a religious center, and the people who run this ashram are followers of Mahatma Gandhi. There is also a clinic at the ashram, where sick people can go to be treated.

Sakina's mother helps Balikaran and her husband by spinning silver thread from a reel onto bobbins. The bobbins fit into the shuttles on the loom. The spinning wheel is made from an old bicycle wheel.

She works in the front room of the house with the weavers and also sells glass bangles there. Ten bangles cost one rupee.

There are two more rooms at the back of the house. One is a storeroom which holds spare parts for the looms. The other room is used as a kitchen and bedroom.

Asharap and Sakina often sit on their bed, called a *charpoy*. It is made of rope netting. Their parents also have a *charpoy*. This kind of bed is light and easy to carry. During the summer, everyone takes their beds outside to sleep under the stars.

Sakina and Asharap watch their mother winnow wheat. She shakes the basket up and down. All of the unwanted stones and pieces of straw are separated from the wheat and tossed out of the basket. When the wheat has been winnowed, she will grind it into flour. Then she will make *chapattis*, a kind of flat round bread. She cooks it in the fireplace, which is in the back room near the back door.

Sakina's mother made the fireplace out of clay. The family burns a mixture of wood and dry cow dung. Wood is expensive because there aren't many trees near the village. The house has no chimney, so the smoke drifts out through gaps in the roof.

The family eats mutton (sheep) or vegetables and lentils with *chapattis* or rice. They buy the rice and lentils at a store, but a woman comes to the house to sell vegetables. To weigh spinach, she places it on one side of her scale and puts a rock on the other side.

One chicken and one goat provide the family with fresh eggs and milk. Asharap's job is to take care of the chicken. Sakina takes care of the goat, but it often gives her trouble. It butts through its rope and runs off to eat the farmers' crops. Sakina had to put a brass bell around the goat's neck to keep track of it.

To feed the goat, Sakina cuts grass from the banks around the sides of the fields and carries it home in a basket for the goat to eat. Usually she goes barefoot, but when the fields are wet she wears her plastic sandals.

Another of Sakina's jobs is to get water from the well. Her family shares the well with ten other families. Each person who uses the well is careful to keep it clean so that everyone can have fresh water to drink.

Although the well is deep, the water level is very low during the dry months of the year. None of the water is wasted, and everyone looks forward to the first monsoon rains in June, when the well will fill up again.

Sometimes Sakina helps her mother wash clothes. She rubs them with a bar of hard soap. Then she scrubs them on a stone slab.

If the sun is out, she lays the clothes out on the ground to dry. When it rains, she hangs them on a line inside the house.

Across the fields from Sakina's house is the house of a rich farmer. He has a modern well with a pump to irrigate his land. Sometimes her family goes over to his farm to wash their clothes and have a bath. It's especially refreshing to bathe there on a hot day, because the cool water comes from deep down in the ground.

When her father finishes weaving, he relaxes by smoking his *hookah*. The *hookah* makes a bubbling noise as he draws the smoke through the water in the bowl of the pipe. The bowl is made from a coconut shell. The tobacco in the clay top is kept lit by pieces of burning charcoal. It is winter, and her father is wearing a woolen vest. The blue cotton garment is called a *lungi*.

There is no TV or radio in Sakina's house. In the evening, her family sings songs and tells stories. Sometimes Sakina and Asharap play a game called *guli danda*. They take turns hitting a small wooden peg with a stick. When the peg is in the air, they try to hit it again and see how far it will go.

Asharap likes to play *pithoo*. It's a team game. He throws the ball to knock over a pile of seven pieces of broken roof tile. Then his teammates try to pile them up again before the other team hits them with the ball.

Every Friday, Sakina's father rides his bicycle to the mosque to pray. The mosque has been built at a crossroads. Muslims come from all the surrounding villages to meet at the mosque. On his way home, her father often buys mutton from a Muslim butcher who has set up his stall at the crossroads.

One year he bought a calendar in Varanasi from a street vendor. It shows a boy reading the Koran, the holy book of the Muslims.

Once a month, Sakina's father travels into Varanasi to sell his *sari* borders to merchants and to buy more thread. Sometimes he takes the whole family with him. They walk along paths through the fields to Sevapuri station, where they have a cup of tea while they wait for the train. The cups are made of clay and are thrown away after they are used.

102837

The train stops at every station and finally reaches Varanasi an hour later.

The children stay close to their parents so that they won't get lost in the big city. The streets are crowded and noisy. Traders shout and bicyclers ring their bells. Tricycle rickshaws and horse-drawn tongas take people from place to place. When they've finished shopping, Sakina's family takes a tricycle rickshaw back to the station.

Varanasi is a famous city. The Ganges River is holy for Hindus, and Hindus come from all over India to bathe in it. There are temples all along the riverbank. Foreign tourists go out in boats to take photographs of the scenery.

The family leaves Varanasi just as the sun is setting. Each of them has something to show the neighbors—Asharap has a toy snake, Sakina has a new pair of plastic sandals, their mother has a bright aluminum cooking pot, and their father has a new *lungi*. As the passenger train clicks across the iron bridge over the river toward Taku-kibowli, Asharap and Sakina fall asleep.

Hinduism: India's Oldest Religion

Sakina, Asharap, and their parents are Muslims. There are about 76 million Muslims in India. By contrast, there are almost eight times as many Hindus (about 575 million) in India.

Hindus worship many gods, and most Hindus believe that these different gods represent different aspects of one universal spirit. The three most important Hindu gods are Brahma, the creator of the universe, Shiva, its destroyer, and Vishnu, its preserver.

Hindus believe in reincarnation; that is, they believe that a person's soul doesn't die when the body dies, but is reborn into another body, either human or animal. Whether someone's actions on earth have been good or evil determines whether the soul will be reborn at a higher or a lower level. This concept is called karma.

Another part of Hinduism is the caste system, which divides Hindus into social classes. Each caste has a traditional set of occupations. Hindus are born into their castes and cannot change them. The four main castes are the Brahmins (priests, scholars, and teachers), Kshatriyas (rulers and soldiers), Vaisyas (merchants and farmers), and Sudras (unskilled workers). Until about 40 years ago, there was also another class of Hindus—untouchables. That class has been abolished, and it is now against the law to discriminate against Indians who were once called untouchables.

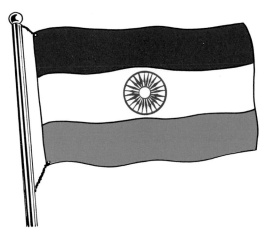

Facts about India

Capital: New Delhi
Official Language: Hindi
  Hindi is one of 14 major languages spoken in India. There are also over 1,000 minor languages spoken there.
Form of Money: The rupee
Area: 1,269,219 square miles
(3,287,263 square kilometers)
  India is slightly less than one-third the size of the United States.
Population: about 724 million people
  India has over three times as many people as the United States. India has the second largest population of any country in the world. Only China has more people. Every year, India's population grows by several million people.

NORTH
AMERICA

SOUTH
AMERICA

EUROPE

A S I A

India

AFRICA

AUSTRALIA

Families the World Over

Some children in foreign countries live like you do. Others live very differently. In these books, you can meet children from all over the world. You'll learn about their games and schools, their families and friends, and what it's like to grow up in a faraway land.

An Aboriginal Family
An Arab Family
A Family in Australia
A Family in Bolivia
A Family in Brazil
A Family in Chile
A Family in China
A Family in Egypt
A Family in England
An Eskimo Family
A Family in France

A Family in Hong Kong
A Family in Hungary
A Family in India
A Family in Ireland
A Kibbutz in Israel
A Family in Italy
A Family in Jamaica
A Family in Japan
A Family in Kenya
A Family in Liberia
A Family in Mexico
A Family in Morocco

A Family in Nigeria
A Family in Norway
A Family in Pakistan
A Family in Peru
A Family in Singapore
A Family in South Korea
A Family in Sri Lanka
A Family in Sudan
A Family in Thailand
A Family in West Germany
A Zulu Family

Lerner Publications Company, 241 First Avenue North, Minneapolis, Minnesota 55401